Lacy Sunshin
Moonbeams and Fairy Tale Dreams Coloring Book
Volume 31

Over 30 Gorgeous Images To Color

Illustrated by Artist Heather Valentin

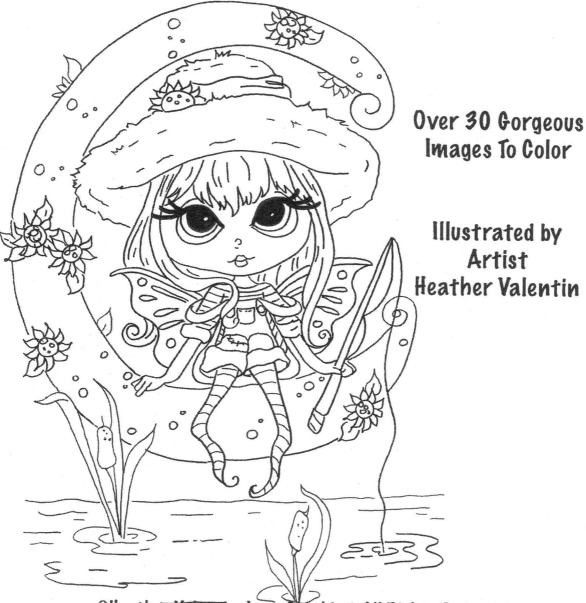

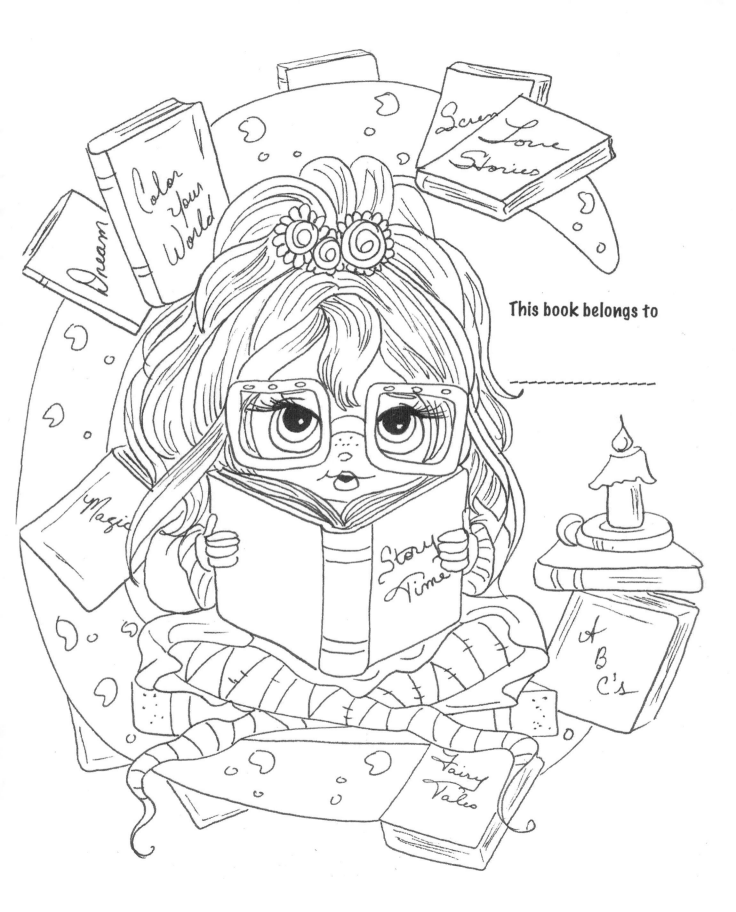

This book belongs to

_____

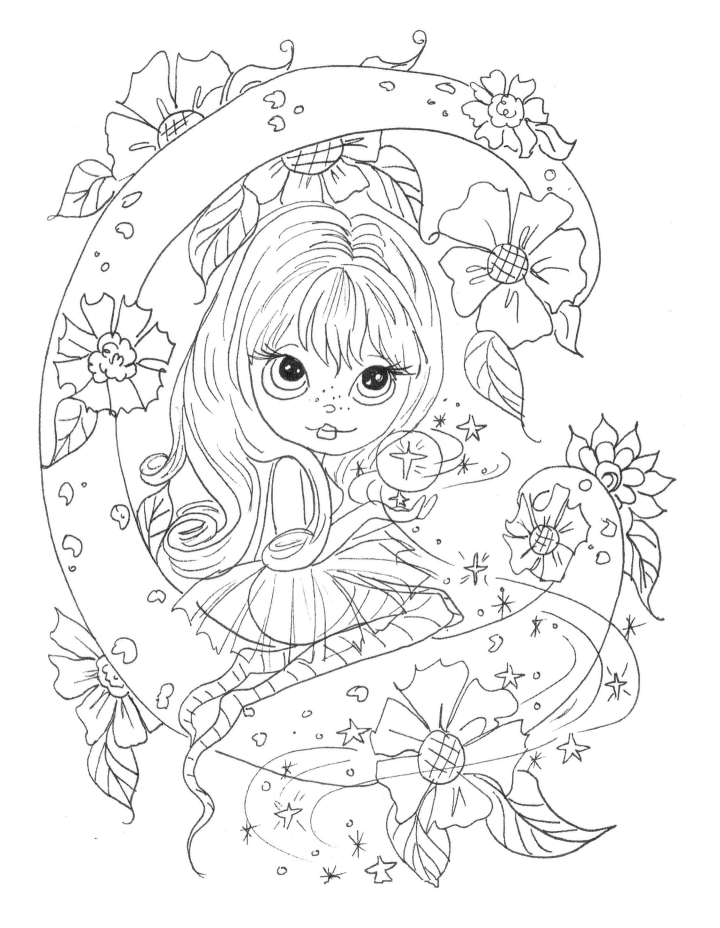

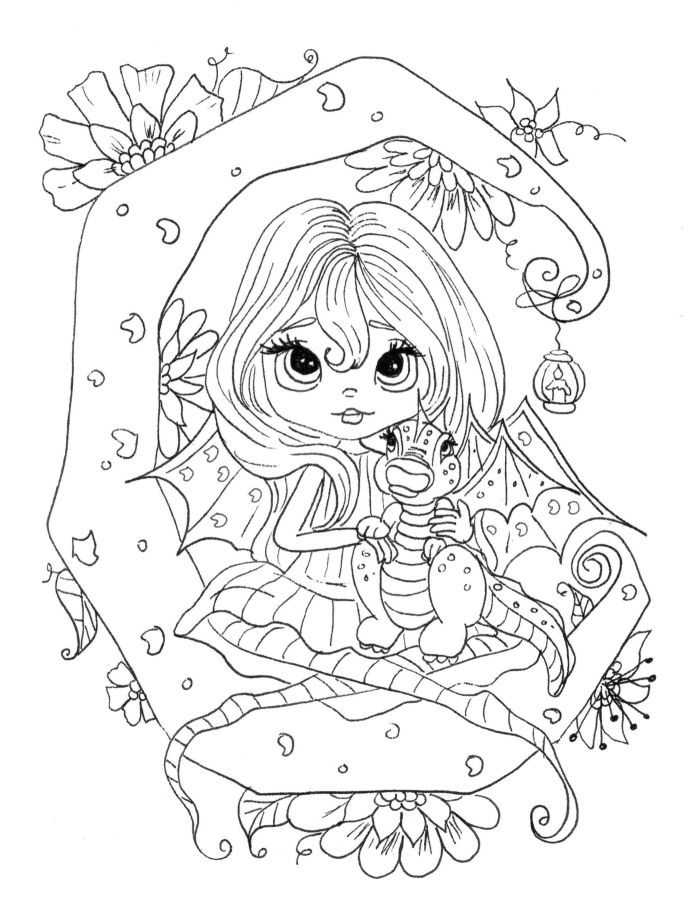

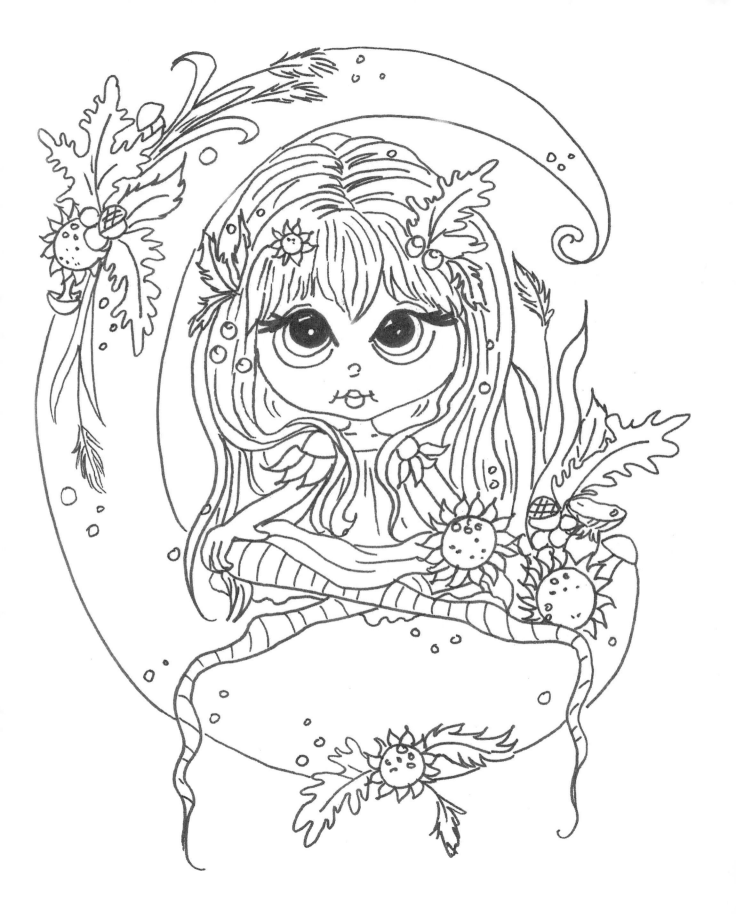

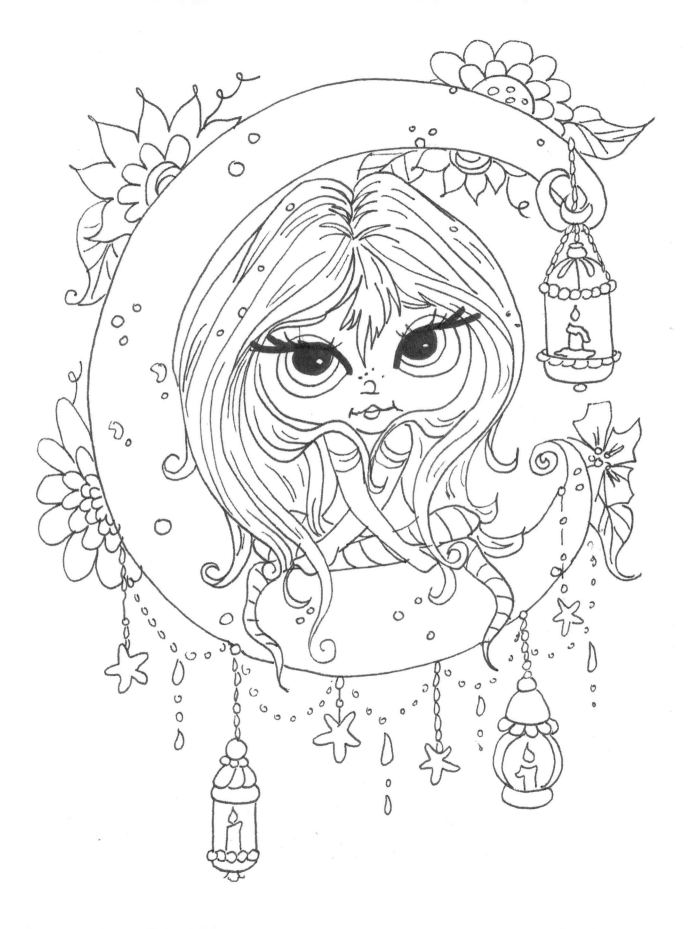

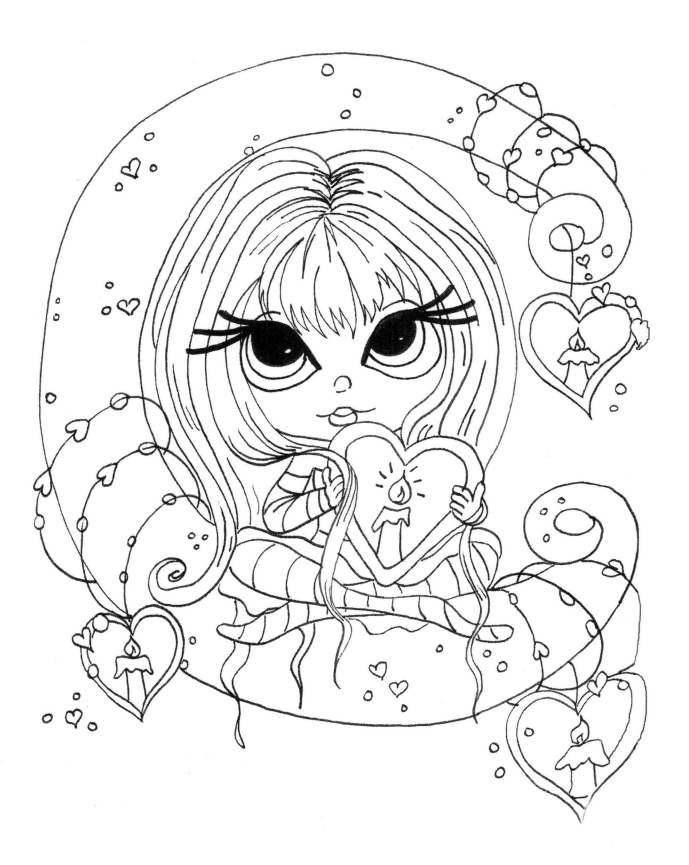

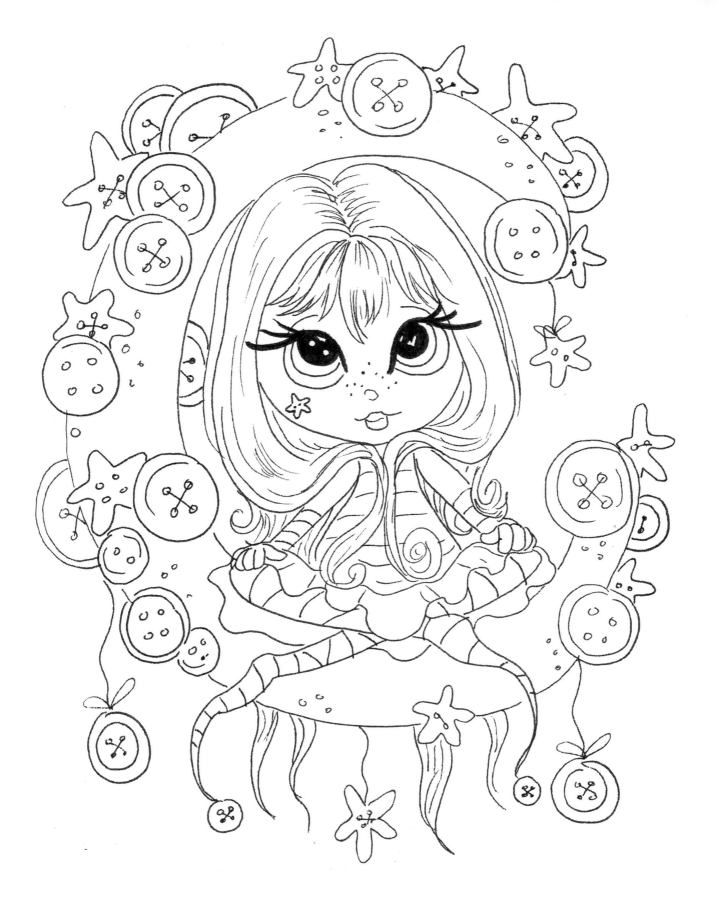

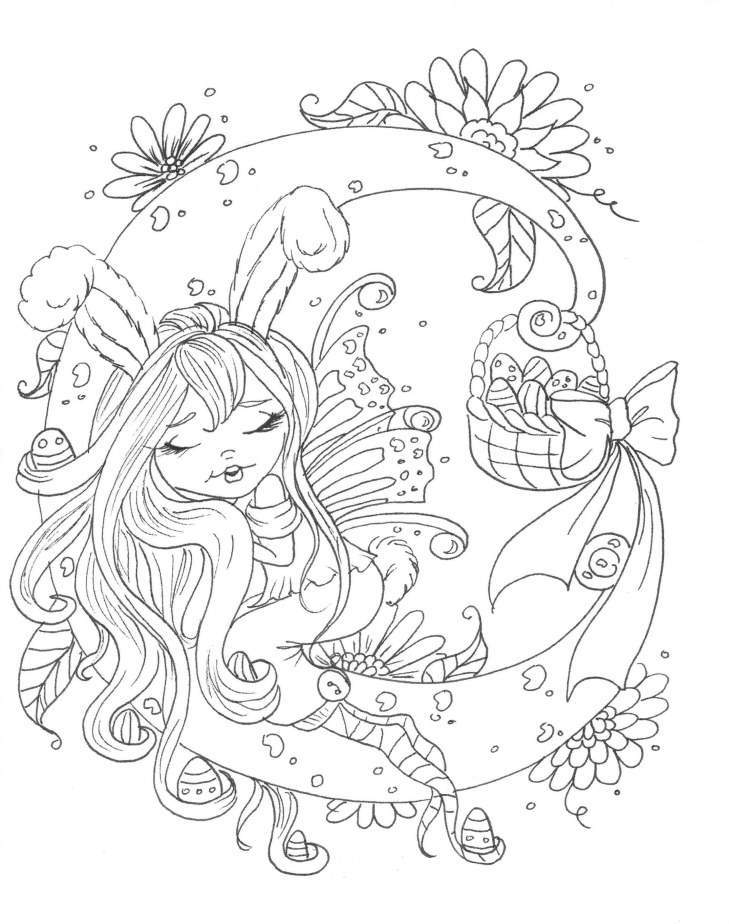

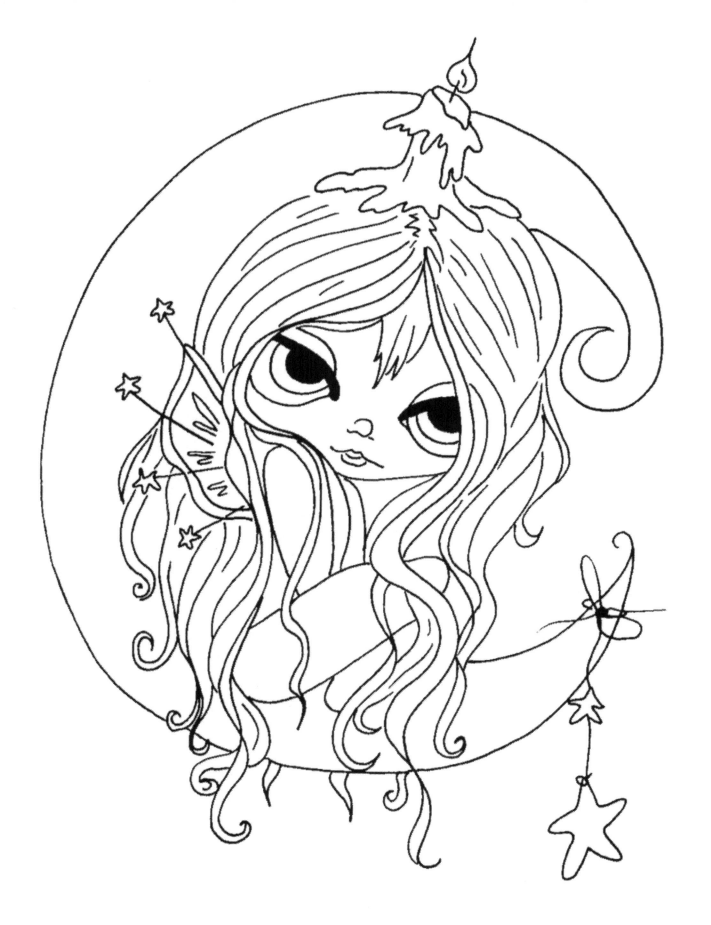

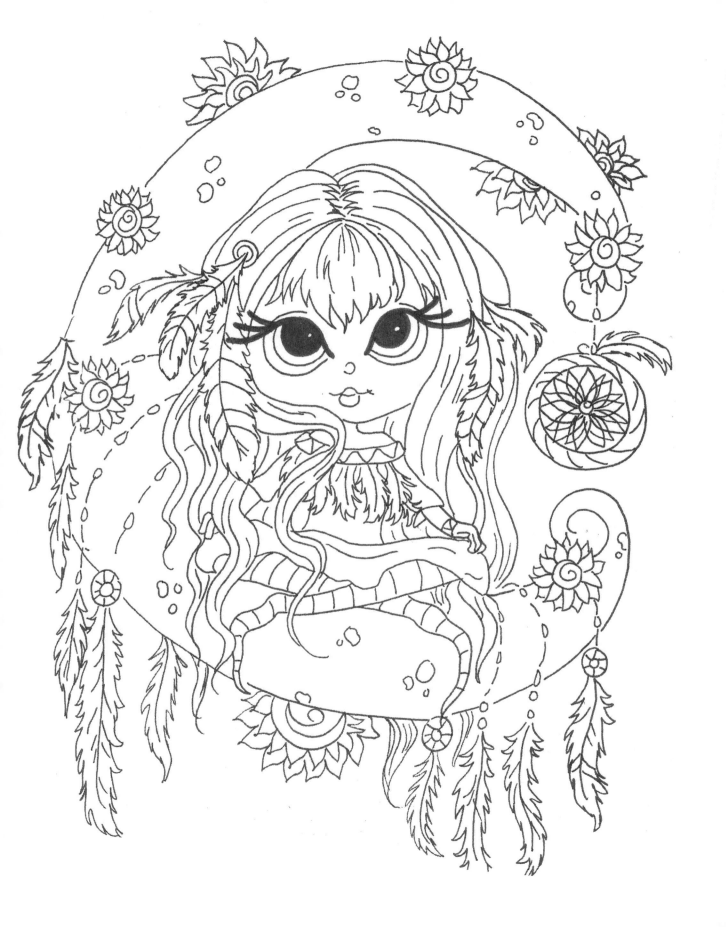

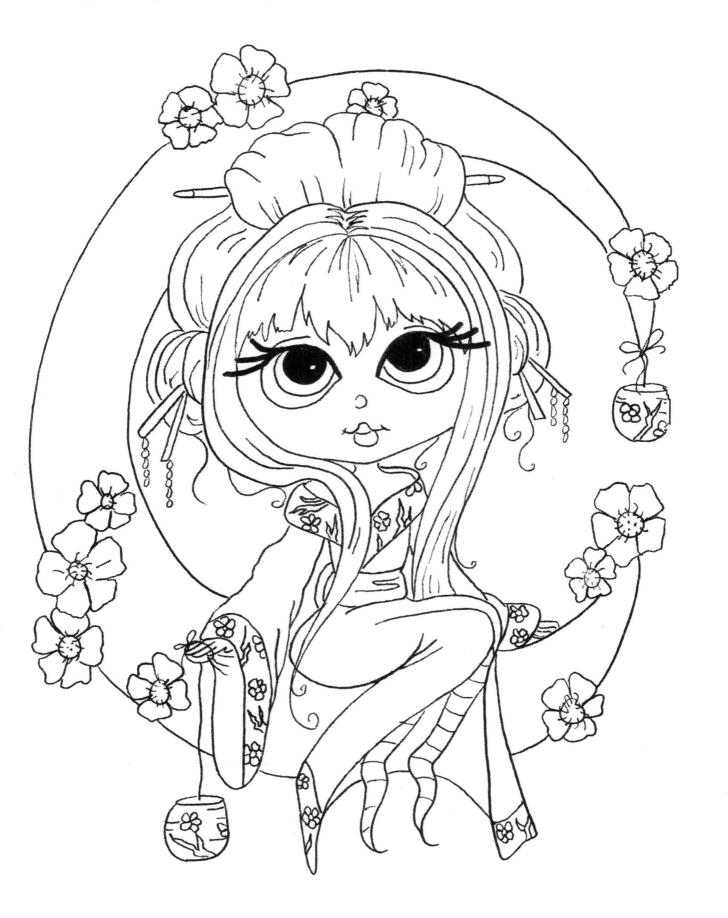

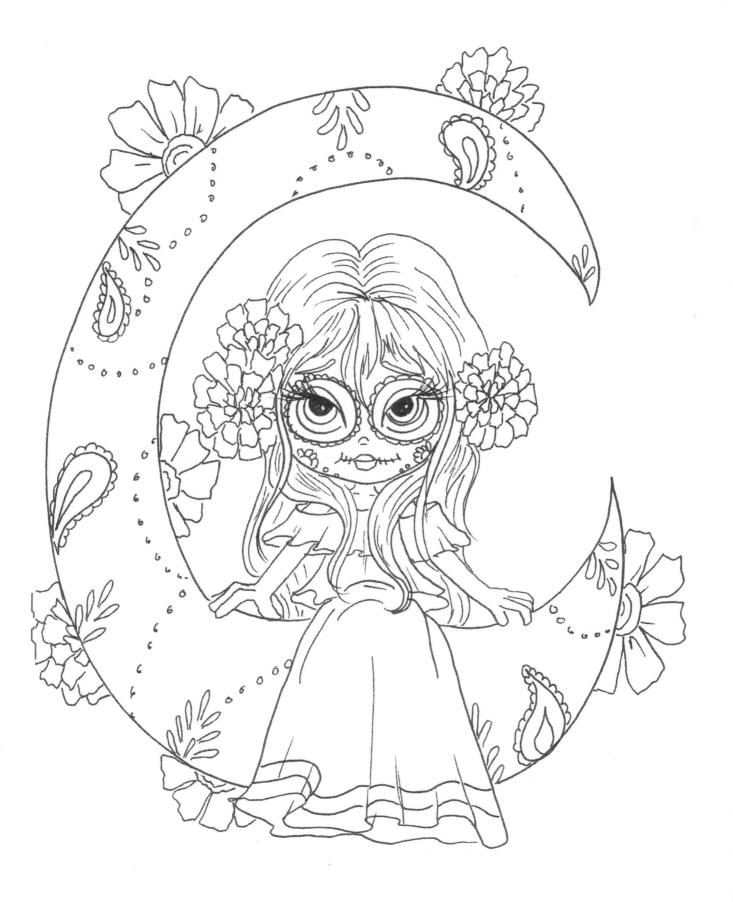

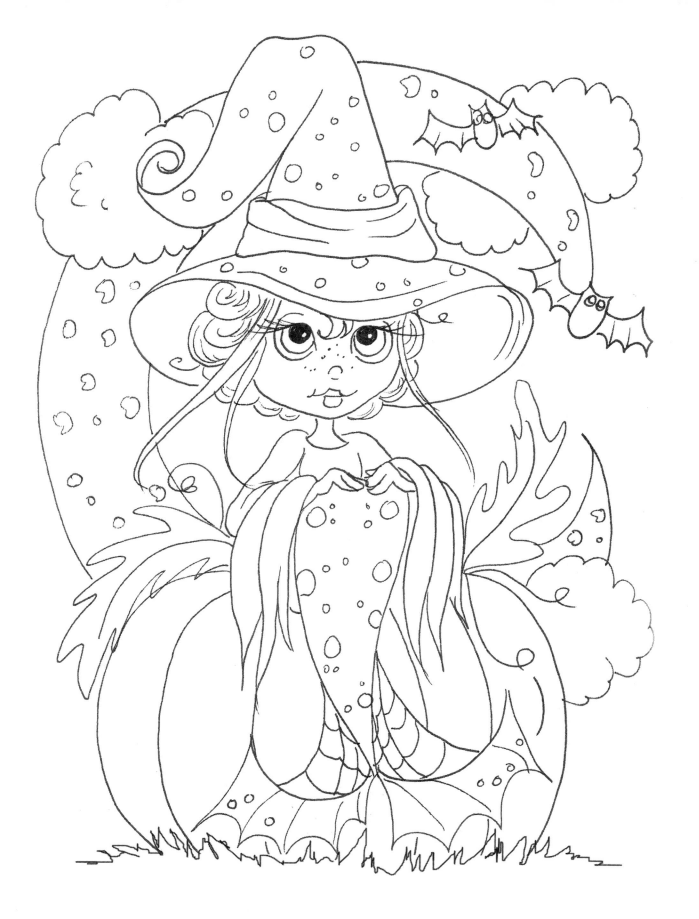

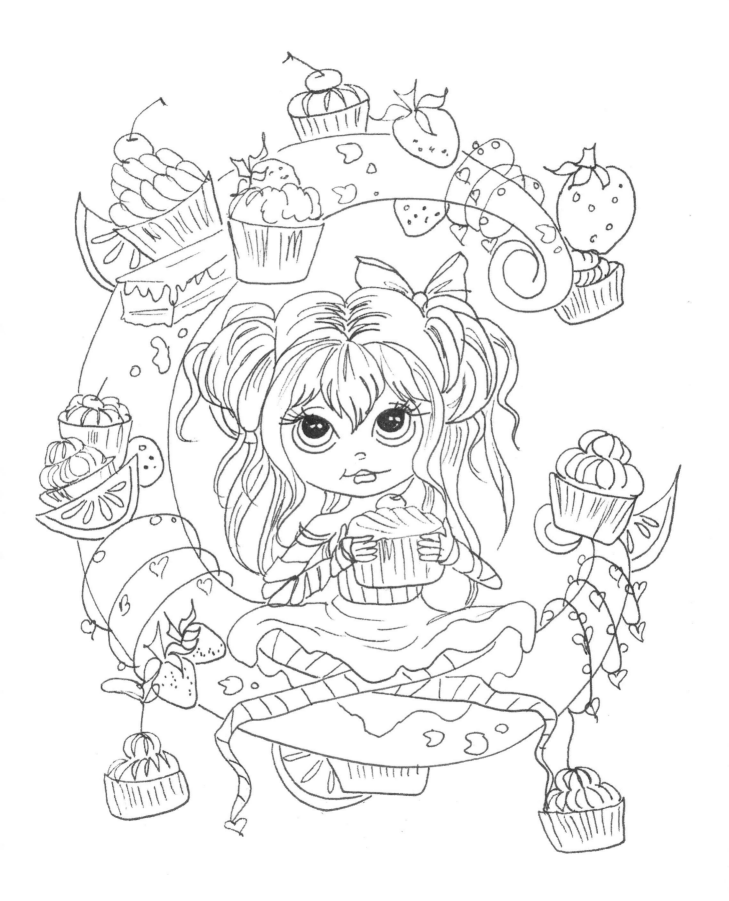

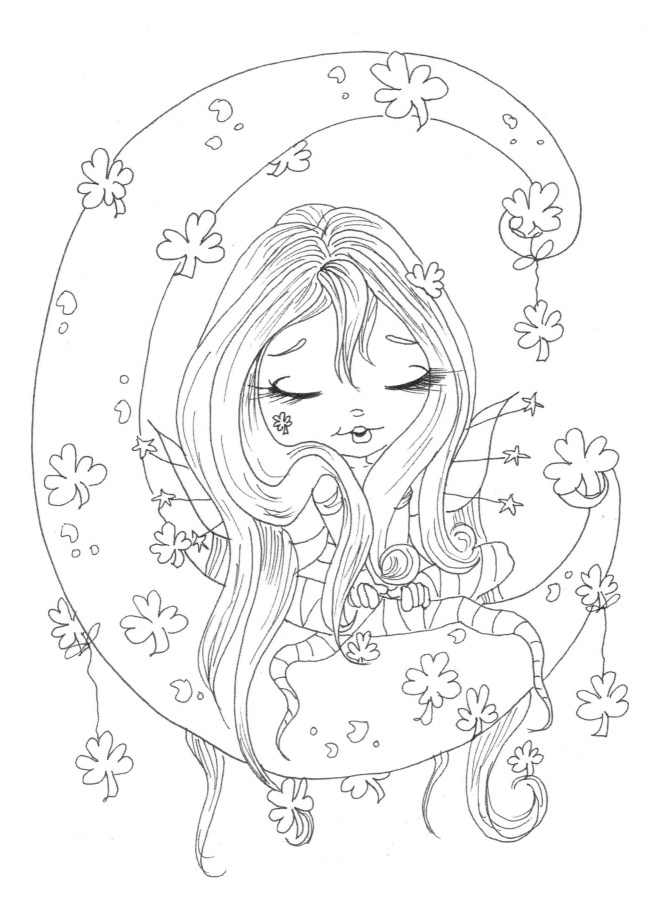

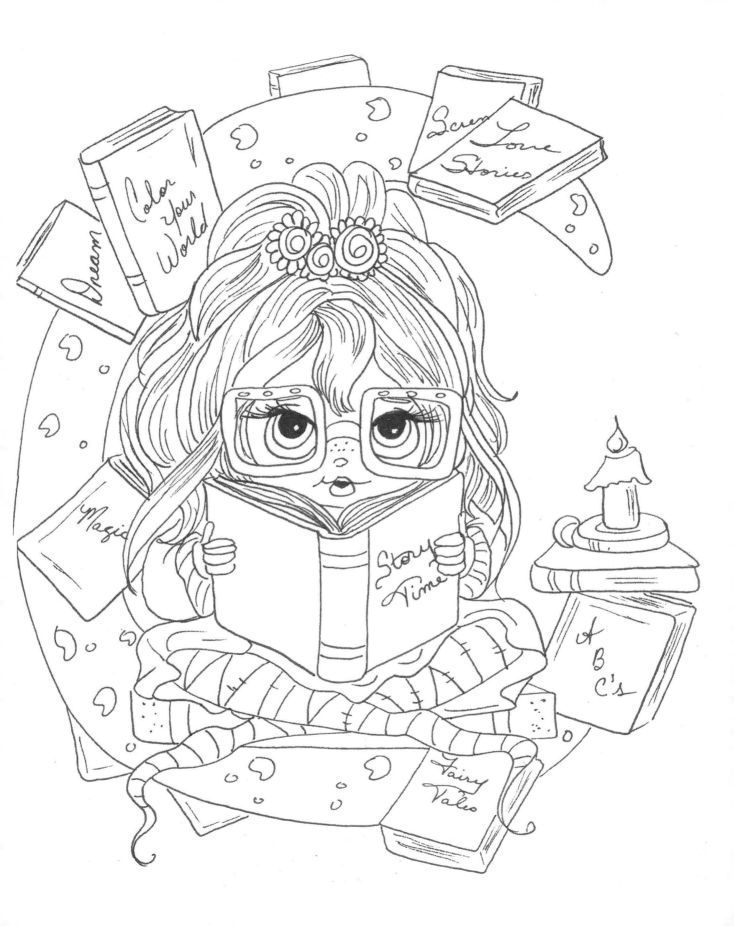

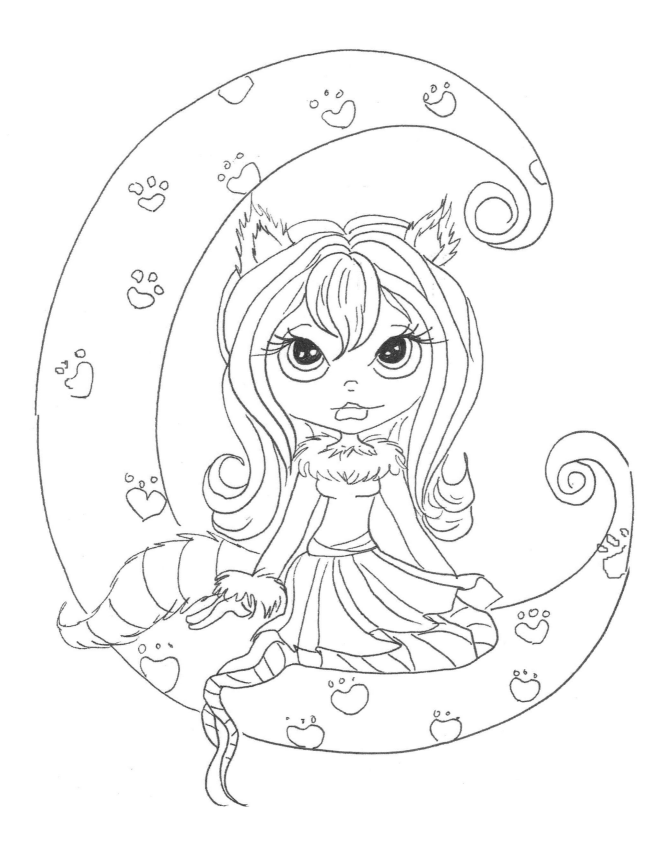

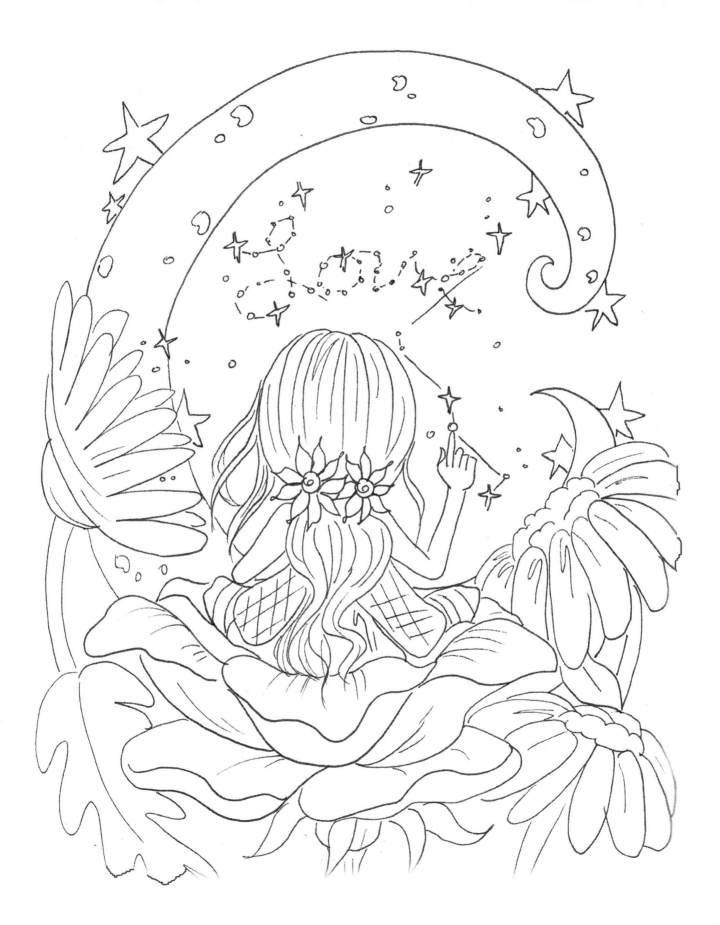

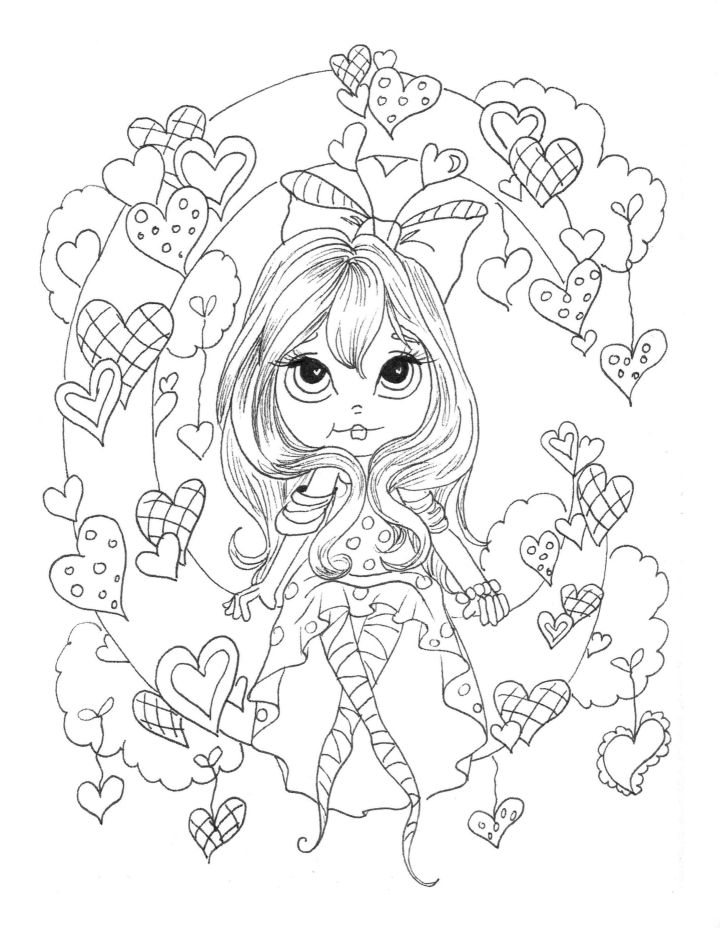

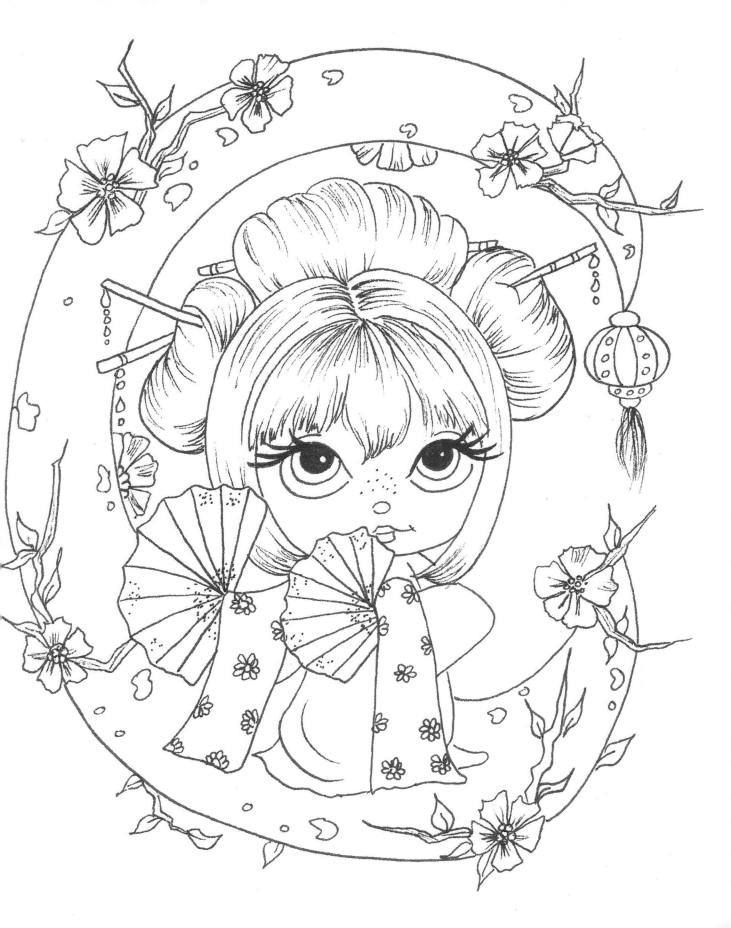

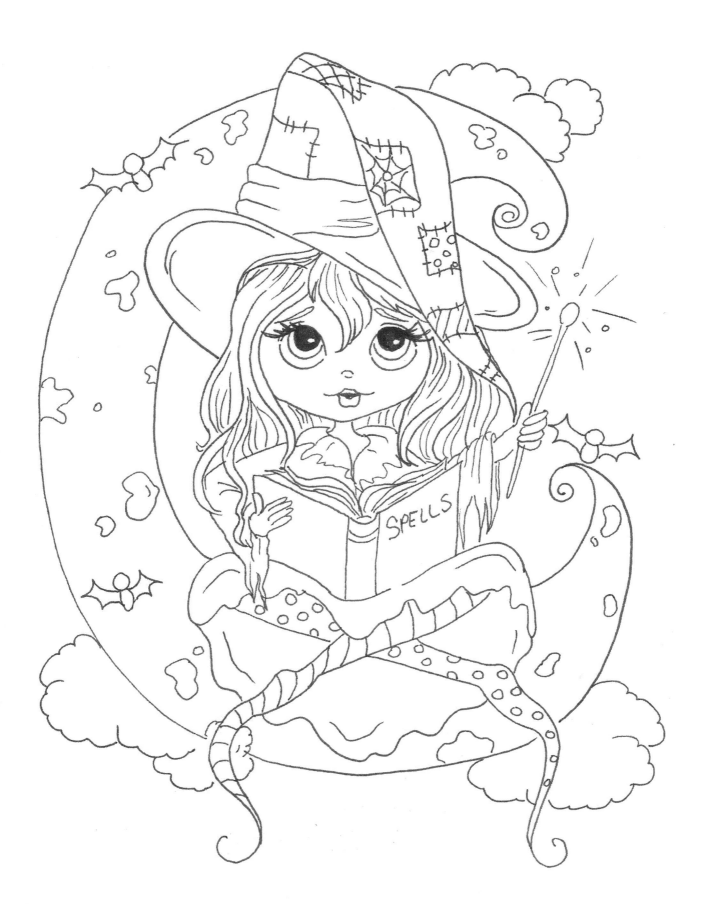

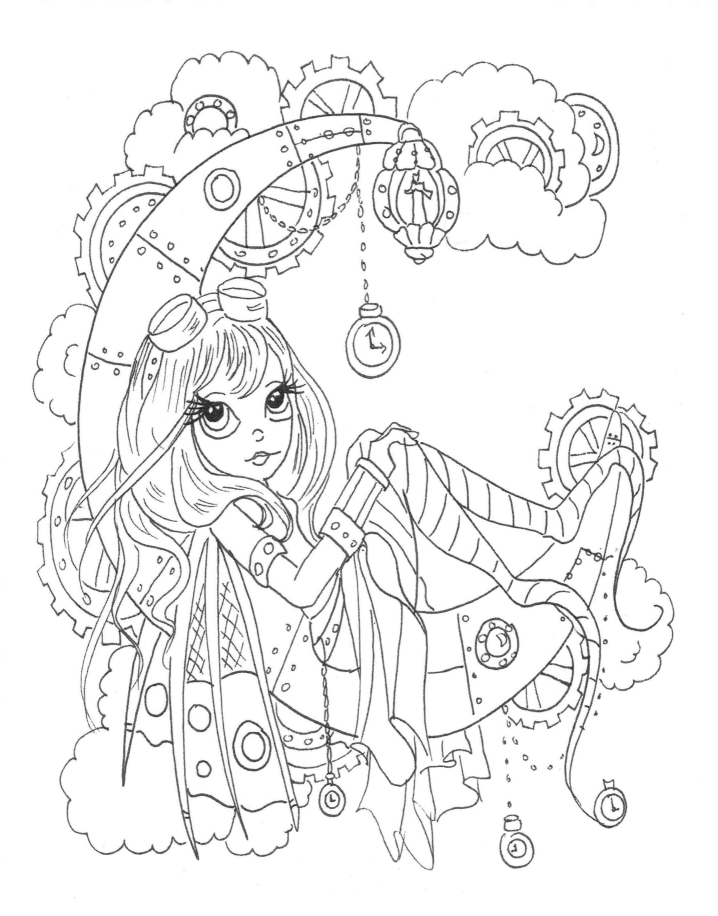

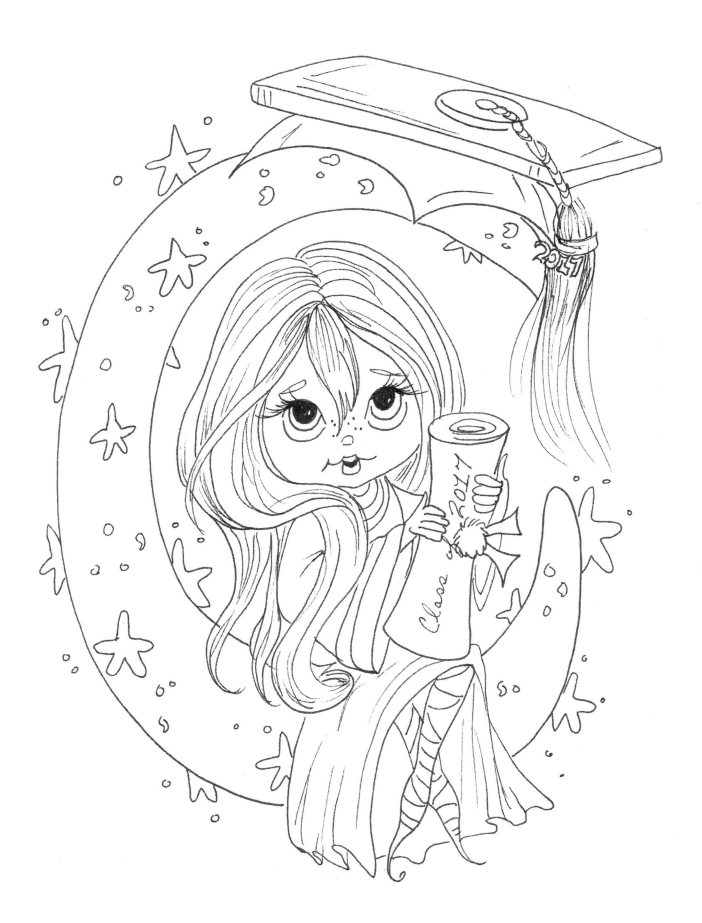

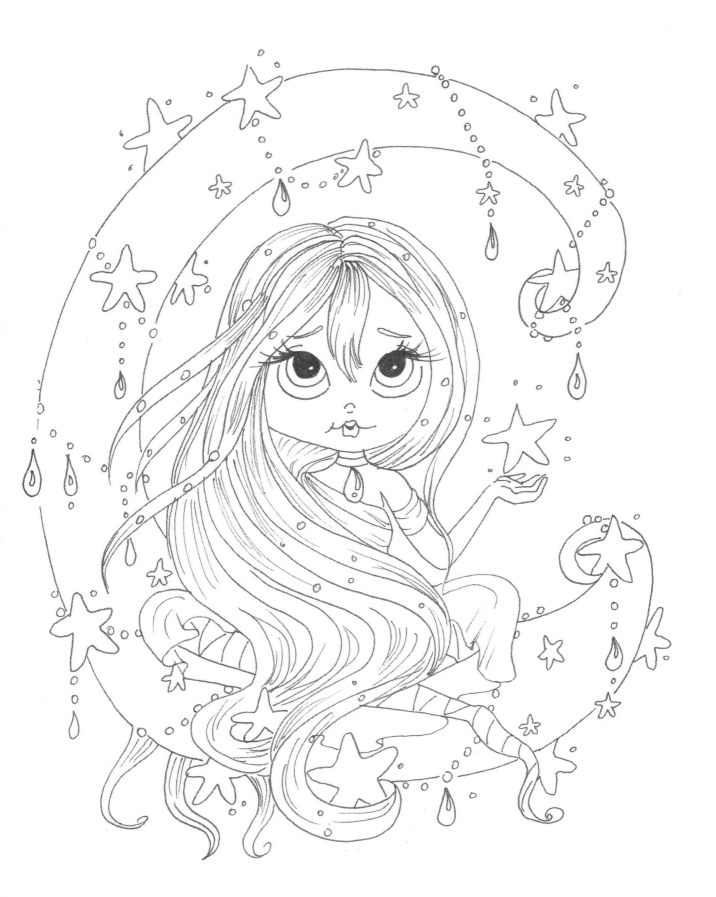

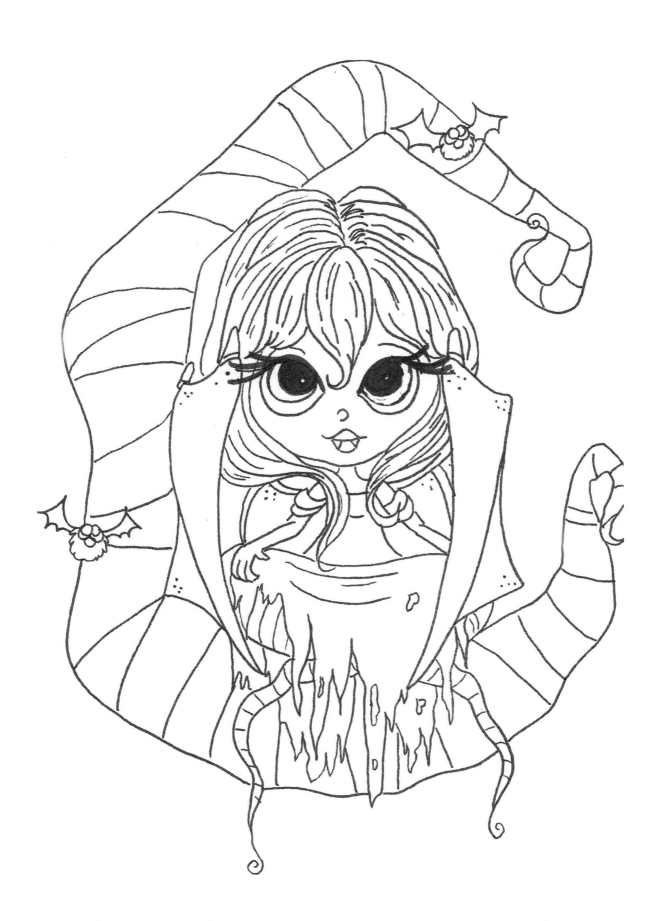

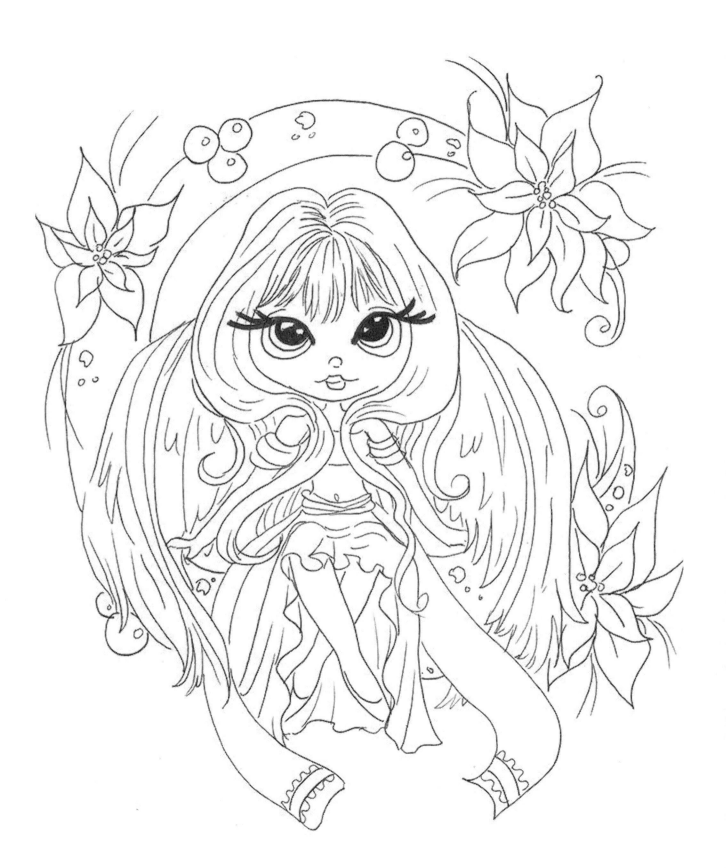

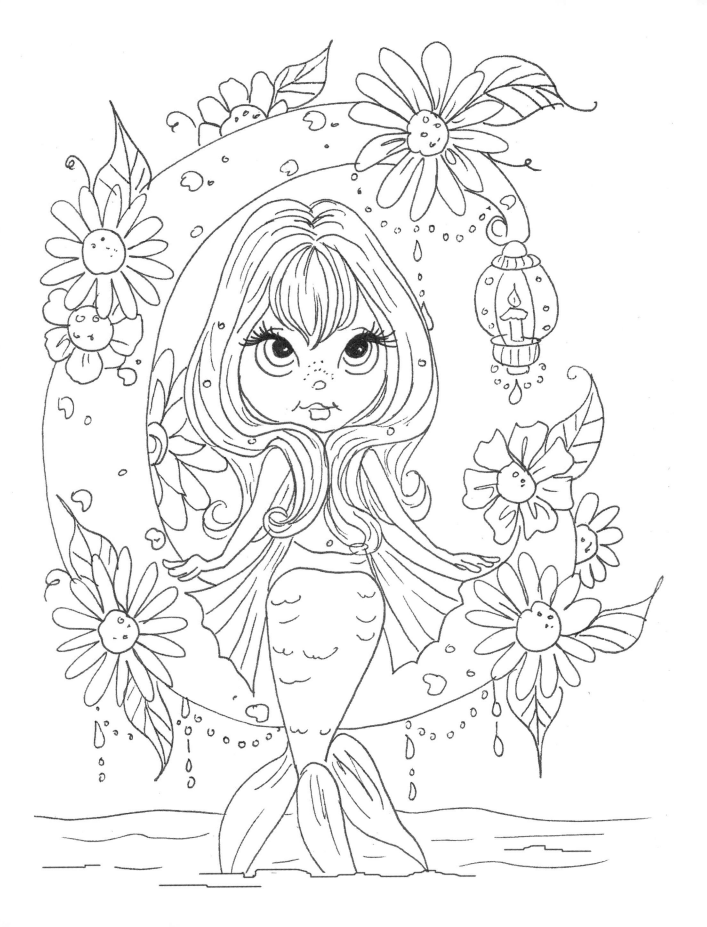

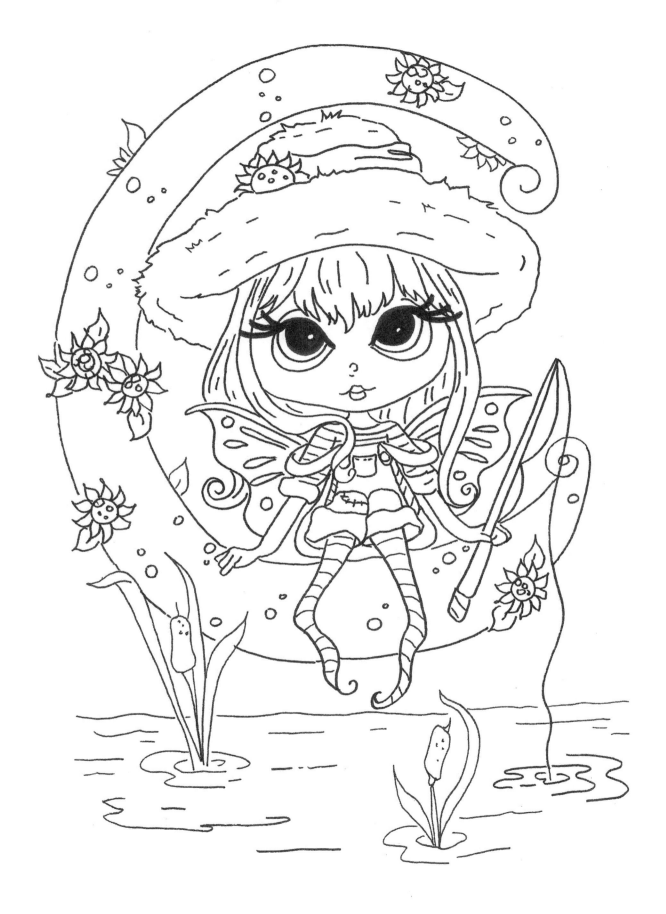

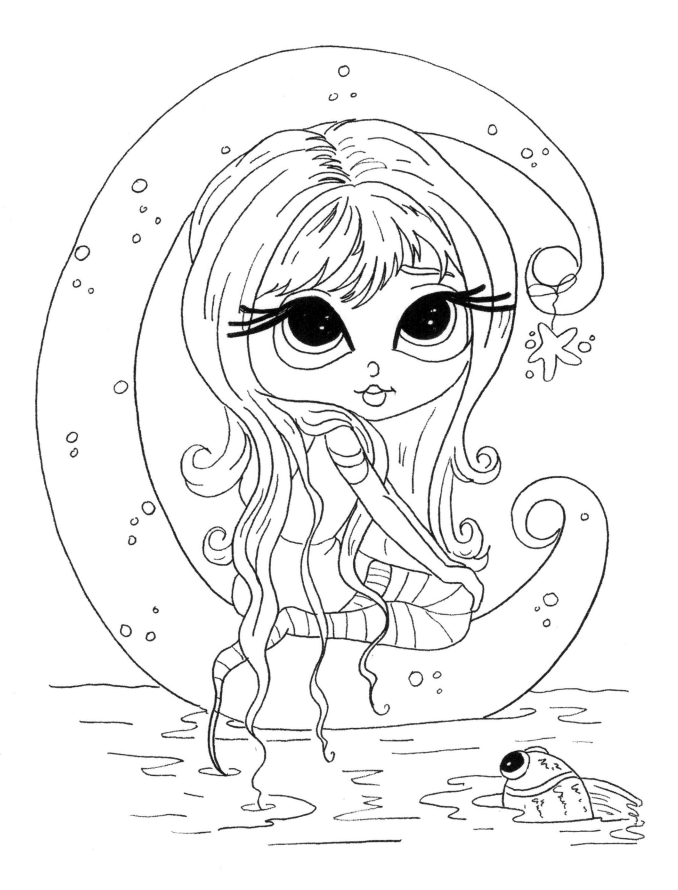

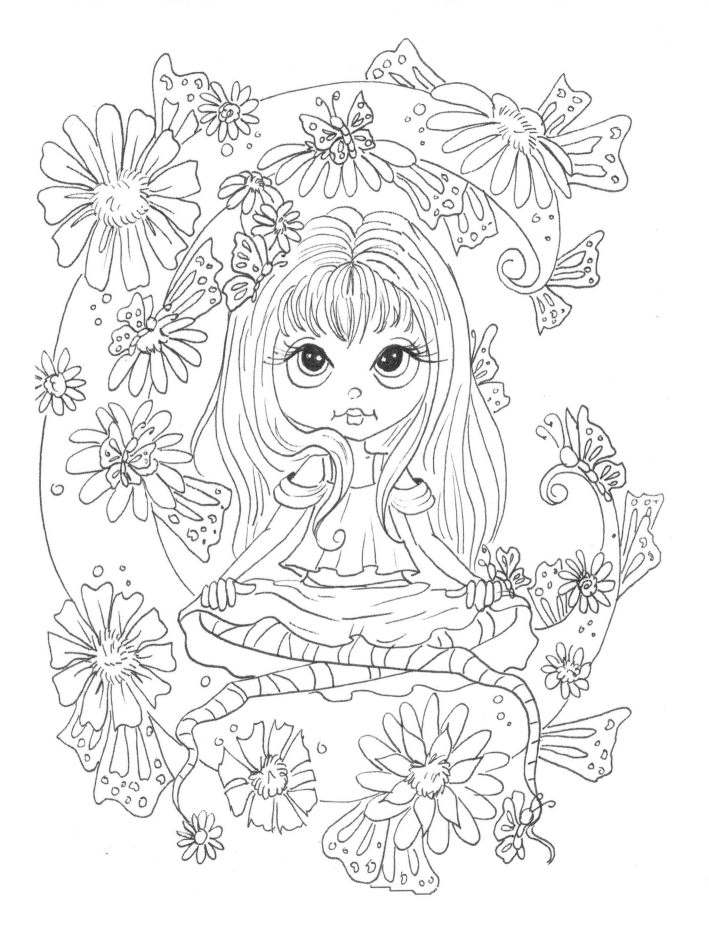

Made in the USA
Lexington, KY
24 September 2017